Mr. Gazoo

A CARTOON HISTORY OF THE REAGAN ERA

TOLES

PANTHEON BOOKS · NEW YORK

For my brother,
George

Library of Congress Cataloging-in-Publication Data

Toles, Tom.
Mr. Gazoo : a cartoon history of the Reagan era.

1. United States—Politics and government—
1981-   —Caricatures and cartoons. 2. Reagan,
Ronald—Caricatures and cartoons.   3. American wit
and humor, Pictorial.   I. Title.
E876.T64   1987   973.927   87-42827
ISBN 0-394-75717-3

Manufactured in the United States of America
First Edition

Picture this. It's late Sunday afternoon; we're already late for dinner. Homework isn't finished. Big test tomorrow. The feeling is like there's somebody behind you with a crane slowly lowering a five-million-pound block of pig iron onto your back. What to do, what to do? There's really only one answer. Borrow a couple of bucks and buy a gigantic hot-fudge sundae.

The above could be a metaphor for the entire Reagan presidency.

Or not. Maybe the Reagan presidency was like a bright new day. A morning. Morning in America. Gee, the sun is bright this morning! And why didn't we notice those birds singing so cheerfully before? There's nothing we can't do. Not with a wallet bulging with crisp hundred-dollar bills. How could we have overlooked those before, too?

No, it was more like Sunday afternoon.

Now picture this. It's late in Reagan's second term. The economy is like an egg balanced on the point of a pin. The environment has probably passed critical thresholds. Wars have a way of popping up in times of trouble. What to do, what to do? At this point there's really only one answer. Borrow a couple of bucks and buy this book. Sit back and enjoy. Then don't say I didn't warn you.

—*Tom Toles*
Buffalo

Set Number 7: Being President

Chad Quiz

WE KNOW YOU'VE BEEN WAITING FOR A **Chad Quiz**

HISTORY

WHICH COUNTRY IS MOST CLOSELY ASSOCIATED WITH CHAD?
- A. LIBYA
- B. FRANCE
- C. JEREMY

MAP PART

1. LOCATE CHAD ON THIS MAP.
2. LOCATE ANYTHING ON THIS MAP.
3. LOCATE THIS MAP.

WHICH OF THE FOLLOWING REPORTS IS TRUE?
- A. "QADDAFI INVADES CHAD" — N.Y. TIMES
- B. "KHADAFY INVADES CHAD" — ASSOCIATED PRESS
- C. "GADDAFI INVADES CHAD" — TIME MAGAZINE
- D. ALL OF THE ABOVE, WHICH IS WHY CHAD IS IN SUCH TROUBLE.

WHICH STATEMENT IS MORE INTERESTING?
- A. CHAD WAS A FRENCH COLONY, SO THE U.S. NEEDN'T WORRY, SINCE FRANCE WILL TAKE CARE OF IT.
- B. VIETNAM WAS A FRENCH COLONY.

TOLES
UNIVERSAL PRESS SYNDICATE
©1983 THE BUFFALO NEWS

MAP PART, PART II
1. HOW MANY OF THE FOLLOWING CITIES CAN YOU LOCATE IN CHAD?
- FAYA-LARGEAU
- OUM CHALOUBA
- GOUKOUNI OUEDDEI
- HISSENE HABRE
- N'DJAMENA

2. HOW MANY OF YOU KNEW THAT REBEL LEADER GOUKOUNI OUEDDEI AND PRESIDENT HISSENE HABRE WEREN'T CITIES?

IT'S BEEN SAID THAT KHADAFY IS CRAZY.
- A. HIS SUCCESS IN CHAD CONTRADICTS THIS.
- B. HIS INTEREST IN CHAD CONFIRMS IT.

NEXT TROUBLE SPOT: INNER MONGOLIA. START STUDYING...

— 9 —

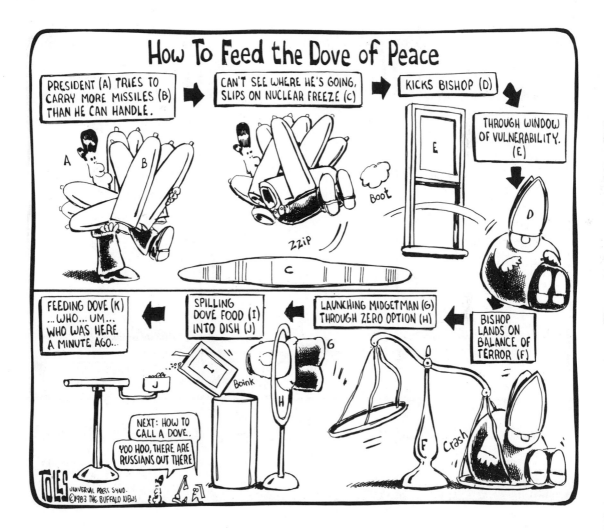

Another Episode of General's Hospital

Taped Highlights of the Latest Press Conference

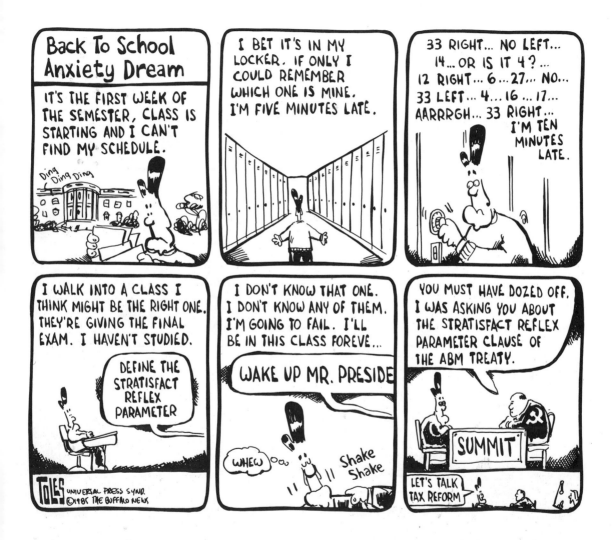

THE SUPERPOWER STRUGGLE REACHES UNCHARTED TERRITORY: CRAYONS

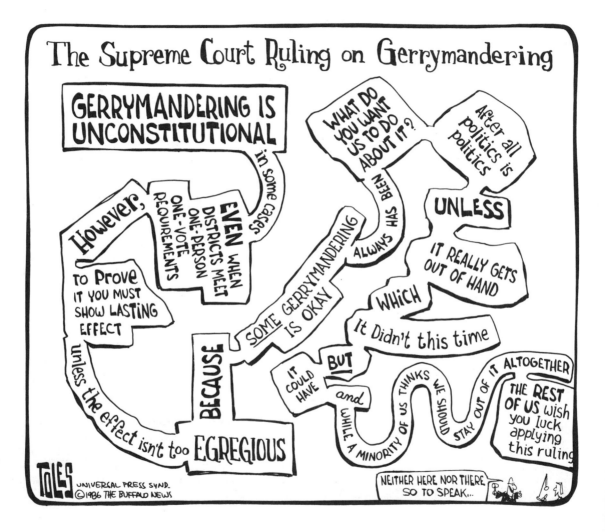

A Summary of the Tax Bill

• a distillation of all that has been written and said about it.

CATEGORY	EFFECT
Lower Incomes	Huge percentage decrease. Dollar amount insignificant.
Middle Incomes	It depends. How do you define middle? What are your deductions? Are you married? Why? Net effect will be about the same.
Upper Incomes	You could get clobbered. But you won't.
Super-Rich	Nothing mortals do applies to you.
Business	Very anti-business, except the pro-growth nature of the bill will offset this.
The Economy	Best thing ever for the economy, though canceled out by the anti-business provisions.
Accountants	Will be put out of work. Right into lavish retirement.

TOLES

ONWARD TO
THE DEFICIT!

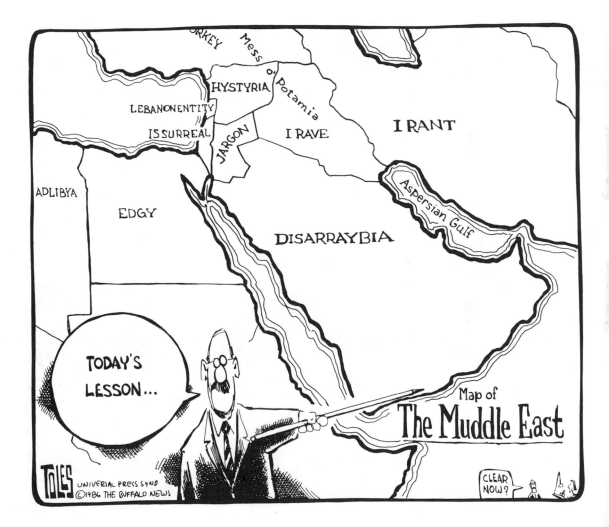

GORBACHEV GOT THE MESSAGE. IT WASN'T AN ARMS RACE ANYMORE.

IT WAS A SPENDING RACE.

AND RUSSIA WAS BROKE.

SO WAS THE U.S., OF COURSE. BUT ONCE THE DEBT PASSES TWO TRILLION, YOU STOP COUNTING.

HA HA HA HA.

SO THAT WAS IT. A SPENDING RACE TO THE DEATH. THE AMERICAN PUBLIC APPROVED.

GO FOR IT!

RECORD DEBT AND CLIMBING

©1986 THE BUFFALO NEWS UNIVERSAL PRESS SYND.

TOLES

SO DID THE JAPANESE.

TOKYO BANK

YEN TO LEND

BORROW YOUR TROUBLES AWAY

COME HERE FOR IT!

..THE LAND OF THE RISING SUM.

The President sends a cake to the Ayatollah and confidently awaits a reply.

...SAME FLAVOR CARTER GOT.

TOLES

Writing Skills Exam. Part 3: Job Application
Write an essay demonstrating your skills at applying for work. Include your background, experience, interests, understanding and competence in the line of work you are seeking.
Whopper
Lg. fries
Med. Coke, no ice
...am. Part 4: Analytical Thinking
My analysis is I'm being realistic
TOLES UNIVERSAL PRESS SYND. ©1986 THE BUFFALO NEWS

1987
Income Tax Simplification
Check all boxes and sign
Occupation:
Lost to imports
Investments:
Stock market crashed
Savings:
Financial institutions collapsed from debt.
Income:
0
Tax:
0
FOLD TWICE, SEAL IN ENVELOPE, PLACE IN POCKET, JUMP OUT WINDOW
©1986 THE BUFFALO NEWS UNIVERSAL PRESS SYND.
TOLES

ORAL ROBERTS CAME DOWN OUT OF HIS PRAYER TOWER TO COLLECT $1.3 MILLION FROM A DOG RACING MAGNATE SO GOD WOULDN'T KILL HIM. THE DONOR SAID MR. ROBERTS WOULDN'T HAVE TO COMMIT SUICIDE NOW, BUT DID NEED SOME PSYCHIATRIC TREATMENT. MR. ROBERTS' SON SAID HIS DAD WAS "TICKLED TO DEATH." MORE LATER.

THE POPE ANNOUNCED SUPPORT FOR LEGISLATION THAT WOULD CAUSE PEOPLE WHO DON'T WANT CHILDREN TO HAVE THEM AND PREVENT PEOPLE WHO DO WANT THEM AND CAN'T, FROM HAVING THEM.

EVANGELIST JIM BAKKER SAID THAT HE RESIGNED NOT BECAUSE OF BLACKMAIL OVER A SEX SCANDAL WITH A CHURCH SECRETARY AS HE SAID LAST WEEK, BUT BECAUSE OF A "HOSTILE TAKEOVER" BID FROM A RIVAL CHURCH. HIS SUCCESSOR, JERRY FALWELL, DREW HEAVY CRITICISM FROM BAKKER'S FOLLOWERS FOR BEING A FUNDAMENTALIST INSTEAD OF A CHARISMATIC.

©1987 THE BUFFALO NEWS UNIVERSAL PRESS SYND.

TOLES

NOW A REPORT ON THE MOVEMENT TO GET RELIGIOUS VALUES BACK INTO THE CLASSROOM...

TIME, CLASS, FOR A POP INQUISITION..

I TOLD THE TOWER COMMISSION I APPROVED THE FIRST IRAN ARMS SHIPMENT.
THEN, THREE WEEKS LATER,
I TOLD THEM I DIDN'T APPROVE IT.
I FELT IT WAS IMPORTANT THEY HAD BOTH SIDES OF THE STORY.
HEY, I'M AS EAGER AS ANYONE TO FIND OUT WHICH IT WAS.
TOLES UNIVERSAL PRESS SYND. ©1987 THE BUFFALO NEWS

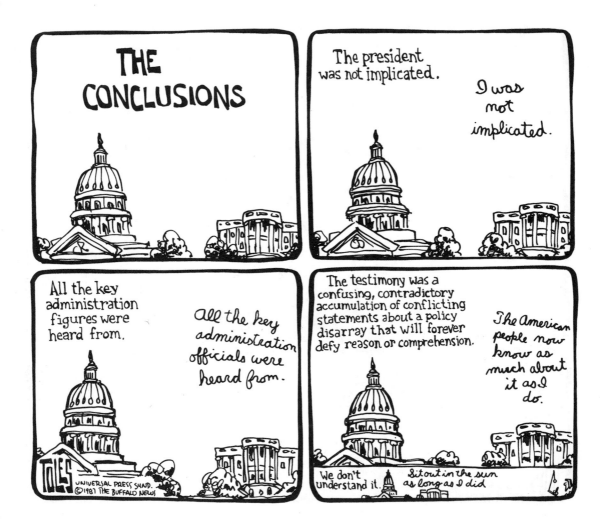

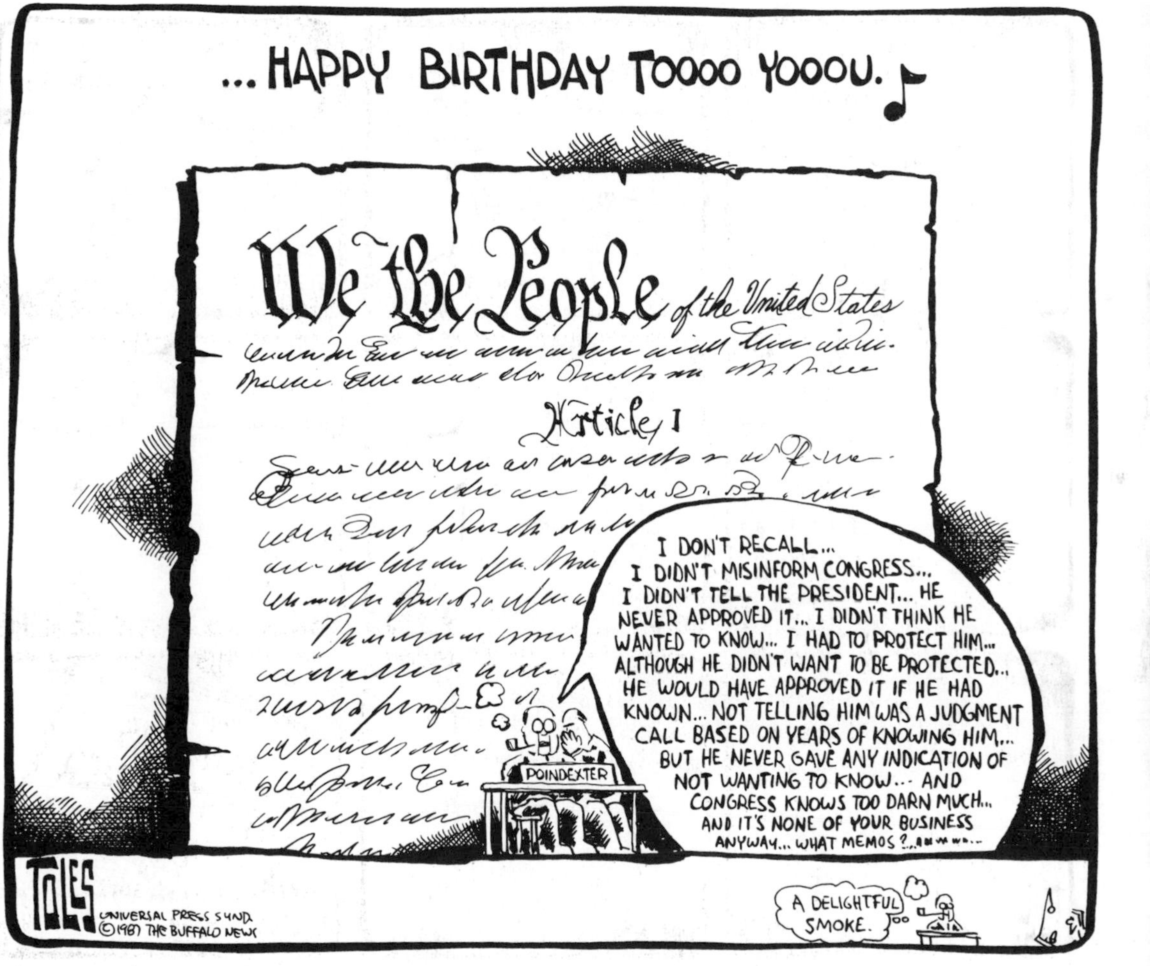
...HAPPY BIRTHDAY TOOOO YOOOU.
We the People of the United States
Article I
POINDEXTER
I DON'T RECALL... I DIDN'T MISINFORM CONGRESS... I DIDN'T TELL THE PRESIDENT... HE NEVER APPROVED IT... I DIDN'T THINK HE WANTED TO KNOW... I HAD TO PROTECT HIM... ALTHOUGH HE DIDN'T WANT TO BE PROTECTED... HE WOULD HAVE APPROVED IT IF HE HAD KNOWN... NOT TELLING HIM WAS A JUDGMENT CALL BASED ON YEARS OF KNOWING HIM... BUT HE NEVER GAVE ANY INDICATION OF NOT WANTING TO KNOW... AND CONGRESS KNOWS TOO DARN MUCH... AND IT'S NONE OF YOUR BUSINESS ANYWAY... WHAT MEMOS?...
A DELIGHTFUL SMOKE.
TOLES
UNIVERSAL PRESS SYND.
©1987 THE BUFFALO NEWS

ABOUT THE AUTHOR

Tom Toles wanted to be a cartoonist who catapulted to prominence from out of nowhere. Therefore he decided to be born in Buffalo. For a father he selected an obscure but kindly freelance writer who had worked for the *Buffalo Times* newspaper until it folded in 1939.

From the moment of his birth in 1951, he (the author, not his father) waited quietly in the shadows of dying heavy industry, biding his time, getting a degree in English, drawing for his college newspaper, and working for the *Buffalo Courier-Express* until it folded in 1982.

He found happiness and job security with the *Buffalo News* (the only paper left in the city), joined Universal Press Syndicate, and catapulted to prominence from out of nowhere.